HACK YOUR BACKYARD

Discover a World of Outside Fun with Science Buddies®

Niki Ahrens

Lerner Publications ◆ Minneapolis

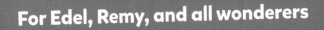
For Edel, Remy, and all wonderers

Official Licensed Product
Lerner Publications Company
A division of Lerner Publishing Group, Inc.
241 First Avenue North
Minneapolis, MN 55401 USA

For reading levels and more information, look up this title at www.lernerbooks.com.

Main body text set in Aptifer Sans LT Pro.
Typeface provided by Linotype AG.

Library of Congress Cataloging-in-Publication Data

Names: Ahrens, Niki, 1979– author.
Title: Hack your backyard : discover a world of outside fun with Science
    Buddies / Niki Ahrens.
Description: Minneapolis : Lerner Publications, [2019] | Audience: Age 7–11. |
    Audience: Grade 4 to 6. | Includes bibliographical references and index.
Identifiers: LCCN 2018014511 (print) | LCCN 2018018316 (ebook) |
    ISBN 9781541543577 (eb pdf) | ISBN 9781541539150 (lb : alk. paper)
Subjects: LCSH: Nature study—Experiments—Juvenile literature.
Classification: LCC QH55 (ebook) | LCC QH55 .A37 2019 (print) |
    DDC 508.072/3—dc23

LC record available at https://lccn.loc.gov/2018014511

Manufactured in the United States of America
1-45098-35925-8/21/2018

CONTENTS

For more information on backyard projects,
scan the QR code below!

YOUR WILD YARD

How well do you know your backyard? All sorts of wild things are going on right outside your door!

A fun way to reveal what is in nature's bag of magic tricks is to hack your backyard. What does that mean? Learn about nature's processes by going outside and exploring the world around you. Find out how the natural world works with hands-on experiments.

Take your curiosity outside, and start noticing the fascinating ecosystem you are a part of. Could you communicate with ants? Or cause a worm to burrow in a new direction? The sky is the limit.

Before You Get Started

Hacking your backyard means you'll be up close and personal with nature. Choose a familiar outside space for each project. You will also need access to indoor storage during a leaf investigation. Get an adult's permission to conduct experiments. Some projects require an adult's help. Be aware of what's around you and how weather or insects might affect your project area.

Many materials can be found at your home, school, or outside. You may need to find and purchase others online or in a hardware store. An adult can help. Gather all the needed materials for an experiment before you begin. Be careful handling materials like glass jars and food coloring outdoors.

Wear sun protection, closed-toe shoes, and clothes that can get dirty when you head out the door. **Let's go!**

WHERE CAN A SEWING NEEDLE POINT YOU?

Make your own compass using a floating sewing needle.

Materials
- metal sewing needle
- magnet
- scissors
- cork
- pliers
- bowl
- water

1. Rub the needle against the magnet 12 times. Move the magnet in the same direction each time.

2. Cut the bottom off the cork, so you have a disc about ¼ inch (0.6 cm) tall.

3. With an adult's help, use pliers to push the needle through the side of the disc. Stop when the same amount of needle shows on both sides.

4. Fill the bowl with at least 1 inch (2.5 cm) of water.

5. Place the cork disc on the water.

6. Rotate the bowl in your hands, keeping the disc from touching the side of the bowl. Which way does the needle point now?

Property of

WHAT'S THE TEMPERATURE, CRICKETS?

Discover how a cricket's chirps can tell you the temperature.

Materials
- evening outdoor temperature of 55°F to 100°F (13°C to 38°C)
- outdoor area with crickets
- seconds stopwatch or timer
- pencil
- notebook
- outdoor thermometer

1. On a warm evening, head outside.

2. Pick out the sound of a single cricket. Use a stopwatch or timer to count the chirps the cricket makes in 14 seconds. Record this number.

3. Two more times, count and record the cricket's chirps made in 14 seconds.

4. Add all 3 numbers, and divide the total by 3. Your answer is the average number of chirps.

5. Add 40 to the average. This number should be close to, if not the same as, the outdoor temperature in degrees Fahrenheit.

6. If measuring in Celsius, count the cricket's chirps made in 25 seconds. Divide this number by 3. Then add 4 to get the approximate Celsius temperature.

7. Check your outdoor thermometer to see how close the crickets were!

SCIENCE TAKEAWAY

Crickets are cold-blooded. Their bodies take on the surrounding temperature. When temperatures get hotter, crickets can chirp faster and more easily. This gives us an idea of the outside temperature without a thermometer.

HOW DOES WATER MOVE THROUGH PLANTS?

Watch colored water move through a plant, and observe how the plant changes.

Materials
- 1 cup water
- 2 empty water bottles or tall plastic cups
- 1 teaspoon blue or red food coloring
- 4 white carnations or other white flowers
- small knife

1. Pour ½ cup water into each bottle.

2. Mix 1 teaspoon food coloring into a bottle.

3. With an adult's help, use a knife to cut the flower stems to 12 inches (30.5 cm) or shorter at a 45-degree angle. (Do not use scissors, as they will crush the stems.)

4. Place 3 flowers in the bottle of dyed water. Place the other one in the clear water.

5. Store the flowers in a safe place where you can keep them for at least 48 hours.

6. After 2, 4, 24, and 48 hours, observe the flowers and leaves. What changes do you see over time?

SCIENCE TAKEAWAY

Water moves from a plant's roots up through its stem and into its leaves and petals in a process called capillary action. By coloring the water, you can see where it traveled.

WHAT SENDS THE ANTS MARCHING?

Experiment with household products to learn if there's a safe, easy way to keep hungry ants away from your picnic.

Materials

- large vinyl tablecloth
- outdoor location with plenty of ants
- bottle cap of water (A)
- bottle cap of half baking soda and half water (B)
- bottle cap of half sugar and half water (C)
- bottle cap of vinegar (D)
- bottle cap of laundry or dish detergent (E)
- bottle cap of hot sauce (F)
- bottle cap of lemon juice (G)
- 7 cotton swabs
- scratch paper
- pencil

1. Spread the tablecloth near ants on the ground, and wait for them to walk on it.

2. Set out your 7 bottle caps, and label them A–G with scratch paper.

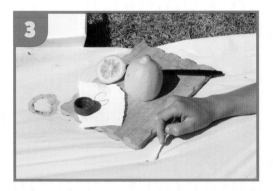

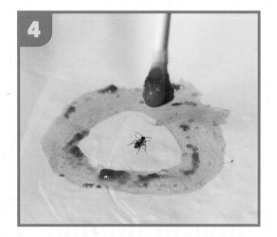

3. Dip a cotton swab into solution A, and use it to draw a 1-inch (2.5 cm) circle around an ant. Repeat with four more ants. Observe whether the ants stay trapped inside or walk out.

4. Repeat step 3 for each of the other solutions, using a new cotton swab for each test.

5. Which solutions trapped the ants inside the longest? Consider using those solutions around your next picnic!

SCIENCE TAKEAWAY

Ants depend on chemical signals such as scents to find their way. Some household solutions have a smell that acts as a negative signal to ants and keeps them away. If ants hesitated to leave a circle, the solution's signal was likely negative. A solution that causes a negative signal is called a repellent.

WHAT COLORS COULD FALL LEAVES BE HIDING?

How many colors are in a leaf?

Materials
- 15 each of 3 colors of soft fall leaves
- scissors
- 3 mason jars
- tablespoon
- isopropyl rubbing alcohol
- wooden spoon
- ultra-absorbent white paper towels
- 9 clothespins

1. Have an adventure gathering leaves!

2. Sort the leaves by color. Snip each group of leaves into tiny pieces.

3. Put each color in its own jar with 2 tablespoons (30 mL) of rubbing alcohol.

4. Select a jar. Crush the leaves into the alcohol with the wooden spoon handle for 5 minutes until the mixtures are dark. Rinse and dry the spoon handle. Then repeat step 4 for the other jars.

5. Put the mixtures in a dark place indoors for 30 minutes. Do not put the lids on the jars.

6. Cut a paper towel into 9 strips, each 1 inch (2.5 cm) wide.

7. Place 3 paper towel strips in each jar, so the ends just touch the alcohol and leaf mixtures. With clothespins, attach each strip to the rim, keeping the strips apart and away from the jar's side.

8. When colors have stopped spreading upward, or after an hour, remove all strips to dry. What colors were hiding, and in what order do they appear?

SCIENCE TAKEAWAY

A plant leaf is made up of a mixture of pigments. We can uncover hidden leaf colors in a process called paper chromatography. This means separating pigments by how easily they travel up the paper.

WHAT IS HOME SWEET HOME TO A BUG?

Build bug habitats, and watch bugs choose their home sweet home.

Materials

- ruler
- 2 or more clean, empty paper milk cartons
- pencil
- scissors
- tape
- notebook
- dry soil
- spray bottle with water
- 12 pill bugs (roly polys), found under stones, old leaves, or in gardens
- timer
- 2 soil additives (leaf litter, untreated wood chips, small rocks, sand, or compost)

1. Use a ruler to measure about 3 inches (8 cm) from the bottom of both cartons. Mark and cut the cartons to this height.

2. Cut a doorway along one side of each carton, about ¾ inches (2 cm) from the base and about 1 to 2 inches (2.5 to 5 cm) high.

3. Put the cartons side by side with their doorways lined up in the middle. Tape the carton bases together tightly, leaving no gaps.

4. Prepare a data table with 3 columns for number of minutes, damp soil count, and dry soil count.

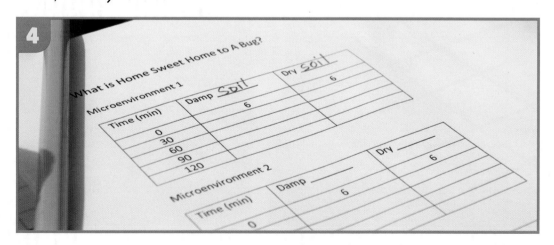

What is Home Sweet Home to A Bug?

Microenvironment 1

Time (min)	Damp Soil	Dry Soil
	6	6
0		
30		
60		
90		
120		

Microenvironment 2

Time (min)	Damp _____	Dry _____
	6	6
0		

Turn the page for more Home Sweet Home.

19

5. Place soil in both cartons up to the doorways. Spray one carton's soil with water until it is damp.

6. You have created a microenvironment, or a miniature version of the pill bugs' natural environment. Carefully place an equal number of pill bugs in each side of the joined cartons. Count the number of pill bugs in each container, and record what they do. Recount every 30 minutes for 2 hours.

7. Repeat steps 5 and 6 to create other microenvironments using materials such as leaves or sand.

8. Read through your observations. How can you tell what microenvironment is home sweet home for these pill bugs? When you finish your experiment, return the pill bugs to their original home sweet home.

SCIENCE TAKEAWAY

Pill bugs are actually crustaceans (like shrimp or crabs), not insects, or bugs. They breathe with gills, so they need a damp environment to survive.

WHERE DID ALL THE STARS GO?

Discover why stars seem to disappear when you're in a busy city.

Materials
- paper towel tube
- markers, stickers, and other art supplies (optional)
- notebook
- pencil
- adult helper
- 3 to 5 locations for star gazing, such as your backyard, a city sidewalk, the countryside, or a campground
- a night without clouds, fog, or a full moon
- flashlight

1. Create your star counter. Decorate the paper towel tube with stickers, markers, or other art supplies.

2. Prepare a data table for recording star counts, location descriptions, and calculations.

3. On a clear night, bring an adult and your materials to your test sites.

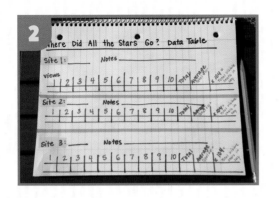

4. At each site, find a safe spot with a clear view of the sky. Write down notes about your location, such as "busy sidewalk by traffic lights," or "dark open space without streetlights." Turn off your flashlight, and let your eyes adjust to the starlight.

5. Point your star counter to one area in the sky. Count each star you see in that area. Record the number in your data table.

Turn the page for more Stars.

6. Move your star counter to view the stars in 9 other areas of the sky. Repeat step 5 for each area.

7. Add the 10 counts. Then divide the total by 10. Record this average in your data table.

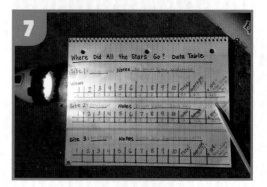

8. Travel to the rest of your test sites, and repeat steps 3 to 7 for each location.

9. Which locations had the most and least visible stars? What could that mean?

SCIENCE TAKEAWAY

The number of stars visible on a clear night is based on how much light pollution, or artificial lighting, disrupts the view. Artificial lighting can drown out the light from the stars, making it harder to see them. Fewer stars are visible in places with higher light pollution.

HOW DO WORMS DECIDE WHERE TO BURROW?

Get to know worms as they wriggle and burrow, or tunnel, through the dirt.

Materials

- pushpin
- 32-ounce clear plastic container, at least 5 inches (13 cm) high
- dirt
- spray bottle with water
- 10 to 15 worms
- newspaper
- cardboard box with cover
- pencil
- notebook
- fine-tip permanent marker
- non-citrus fruit pieces

1. Use a pushpin to carefully poke 4 holes in the bottom of the container.

2. Fill the container with loose dirt. Spray with water. Worms need moist (not soaked) soil.

3. Gently place the worms in the dirt. Worms shy away from light. Do you see them burrow? Top with damp newspaper.

4. Put the container in the box and close it. The box protects the container from light but not from fresh air. Store the box in 60°F to 75°F (16°C to 24°C) shade for two weeks (14 days). Each day, spray with water as needed to moisten the soil.

5. On days 3, 6, and 9, observe and record how many worms and burrows you see and their locations. Trace along the worm burrows with a marker. Do the burrows change over time?

Turn the page for more Worms.

6. On day 9, bury the fruit against the side of the container.

7. On day 10, observe and record the worms' burrowing activity. Did the burrowing pattern change?

8. On days 12 and 14, observe and record what has happened with the worms, the fruit, and the burrows. What do you think causes the worms to burrow where they do?

9. Return the worms to their home in nature.

SCIENCE TAKEAWAY

Earthworms like to burrow. Fresh fruit does not attract worms, but decaying fruit does. As the fruit decayed, the worms burrowed toward the fruit to eat it.

WHAT'S NEXT?

When you've finished these projects, return any living creatures to their original homes. Put away supplies you used, leaving outdoor locations as clean and natural as when you arrived.

You can find extraordinary things when you know where to look. How else might you explore light pollution? Maybe you want to study other creatures' homes or Earth's magnetic field. There's no end to the science you can explore outside!

Imagine how you could hack your schoolyard or neighborhood park next. And when you do, you might find a result or answer that no one else has. Wonder can change the world!

For more information on backyard projects,
scan the QR code below!

GLOSSARY

capillary action: the ability of liquid to flow without gravity in a narrow space

decay: to rot or break down

hack: to go into a system, such as a computer or backyard, to learn about it and get information

light pollution: artificial lighting that disrupts natural views of the night sky

microenvironment: a small-scale physical environment surrounding an organism that is similar to its larger environment

observation: something you have noticed by watching carefully

paper chromatography: a method used to separate colored chemicals or substances

pigment: a substance that gives color to something

signal: a message from one living being or object to another

solution: a liquid mixture of two or more substances

thermometer: a tool that measures temperature

FURTHER INFORMATION

For more information and projects, visit Science Buddies at https://www.sciencebuddies.org/.

Brown, Renata Fossen. *Gardening Lab for Kids*. Beverly, MA: Quarry Books, 2014.
Grow and create in nature with fifty-two fun plant-related activities.

Cornell, Kari. *Dig In! 12 Easy Gardening Projects Using Kitchen Scraps*. Minneapolis: Millbrook Press, 2018.
Grow your own fruits and vegetables using nothing but kitchen scraps.

Oxlade, Chris. *Be an Explorer*. Minneapolis: Hungry Tomato, 2016.
Navigate the wild by using nature's resources in these tried-and-tested outdoor activities.

INDEX

PHOTO ACKNOWLEDGMENTS

Photo credit: Niki Ahrens. Additional credits: ifong/Shutterstock.com, p. 1 (soil); Anna Grishenko/
Shutterstock.com, pp. 2–3; Hero Images/Getty Images, pp. 4–5; Evgeniy Ayupov/Shutterstock.
com, p. 5 (ant); kzww/Shutterstock.com, p. 5 (worm); Letterberry/Shutterstock.com, p. 6 (leaves);
omgimages/iStocky/Getty Images, p. 6 (children); asharkyu/Shutterstock.com, p. 6 (ants); P Maxwell
Photography/Shutterstock.com, p. 7 (food coloring); Halfdark/Getty Images, p. 7 (boy); FatCamera/
E+/Getty Images, p. 7 (girl); ARIMAG/Shutterstock.com, p. 7 (shoe); netsuthep/Shutterstock.com,
p. 11 (crickets); kingfisher/Shutterstock.com, p. 15 (ant); Maksim Shmeljov/Shutterstock.com, p. 16
(autumn leaves); 24Novembers/Shutterstock.com, p. 17 (leaves); yaninaamira/Shutterstock.com,
p. 21 (pill bugs); DAVID NUNUK/Science Photo Library/Getty Images, p. 25; schankz/Shutterstock.
com, p. 26 (worms); Peyker/Shutterstock.com, p. 29; Steven Puetzer/Photolibrary/Getty Images,
p. 30. Design elements: Dreamzdesigners/Shutterstock.com; Ivsanmas/Shutterstock.com; Leyasw/
Shutterstock.com; ScofieldZa/Shutterstock.com; Pinkyone/Shutterstock.com; Dado Photos/
Shutterstock.com; Bob Pool/Shutterstock.com; Anton-Burakov/Shutterstock.com; Tama2u/
Shutterstock.com; iadams/Shutterstock.com; Zephyr_p/Shutterstock.com.

Cover: Letterberry/Shutterstock.com (leaves); ifong/Shutterstock.com (soil); Mama Belle Love kids/
Shutterstock.com (hands); Ivsanmas/Shutterstock.com (ruler); Dreamzdesigners/Shutterstock.com
(ants); Leyasw/Shutterstock.com (canvas); Evgeny Parushin/Shutterstock.com (cricket); Pinkyone/
Shutterstock.com (shovel); kazzpix/Shutterstock.com (pliers); Dado Photos/Shutterstock.com (pliers).